READING POWER

School Activities

Cheerleading

Rae Emmer

The Rosen Publishing Group's
PowerKids Press™
New York

Published in 2002 by The Rosen Publishing Group, Inc.
29 East 21st Street, New York, NY 10010

Copyright © 2002 by The Rosen Publishing Group, Inc.

All rights reserved. No part of this book may be reproduced in any form without permission in writing from the publisher, except by a reviewer.

First Edition

Book Design: Christopher Logan

Photo Credits: Maura Boruchow

Emmer, Rae.
Cheerleading.
   p. cm. – (School activities)
Includes bibliographical references and index.
ISBN: 978-1-4358-3683-9
1. Cheerleading–Juvenile literature. [1. Cheerleading.] I. Title.
II. School activities (New York, N.Y.)
LB3635 .E44 2001
791.6'4-dc21
                                        2001000162

Manufactured in the United States of America

Contents

My School	4
Warming Up	8
Learning Cheers	12
Working Together	16
Glossary	22
Resources	23
Index	24
Word Count	24
Note	24

My School

I love my school.
I love cheerleading.

I like to cheer for my school.

Warming Up

We do some warm-ups when we start.

The coach helps us learn new moves.

Learning Cheers

We learn the words to the cheers.

We learn new steps.

Working Together

We do things together.

The fans cheer with us.

We are a team. We like being cheerleaders.

Glossary

cheer (**cheer**) to call out support for a team

cheerleading (**cheer**-lee-dihng) organized cheering in a group

coach (**kohch**) someone who teaches or trains athletes

warm-ups (**worm** uhps) exercises you do before a game

Resources

Books

The Most Excellent Book of How to Be a Cheerleader
by Bob Kiralfy
Millbrook Press (1997)

Ultimate Cheerleading
by Kieran Scott
Scholastic Inc. (1998)

Web Site

The Cheer Starts Here
http://www.geocities.com/Colosseum/8339/

Index

C
cheer, 6, 18
cheerleading, 4
cheers, 12
coach, 10

F
fans, 18

S
school, 4, 6
steps, 14

T
team, 20

W
warm-ups, 8

Word Count: 56

Note to Librarians, Teachers, and Parents

If reading is a challenge, Reading Power is a solution! Reading Power is perfect for readers who want high-interest subject matter at an accessible reading level. These fact-filled, photo-illustrated books are designed for readers who want straightforward vocabulary, engaging topics, and a manageable reading experience. With clear picture/text correspondence, leveled Reading Power books put the reader in charge. Now readers have the power to get the information they want and the skills they need in a user-friendly format.